NATE CLASSIC READ

Hardy's Wessex Tales

written and devised by
Judith Atkinson

Series editor: Robert Protherough

The *Classic Reading series* is published jointly by the National Association for the Teaching of English (NATE), the UK subject teacher association for all aspects of the teaching of English from pre-school to university, and York Publishing Services Ltd.

NATE
50 Broadfield Road
Sheffield S8 0XJ

Tel: 0114 255 5419
Fax: 0114 255 5296
E-mail: nate.hq@campus.bt.com

British Library Cataloguing in Publication data. A catalogue record for this book is available from the British Library.

ISBN 0 901291 72 2

Design by Black Dog Design, Buckingham
Printed in the United Kingdom by York Publishing Services Ltd,
64 Hallfield Road, Layerthorpe, York YO31 7QZ

Contents

Acknowledgements

We are grateful to the following for permission to reproduce photographs and illustrations.

Dr Gregory Stevens Cox, editor of *The Thomas Hardy Year Book* and owner of the copyright of the collection and works of the late Hermann Lea, pages 1 *left*, 4, 15 and 17 *right*.

Hulton Getty Images, page 1 *right*.

The National Museums & Galleries of Wales, page 17 *left*.

The Folio Society, pages 23 and 29: wood engravings by Peter Reddick from Thomas Hardy, *Wessex Tales* 1987. (© The Folio Society Ltd, London).

Mary Evans Picture Library, page 28 *top left*.

Anthony Jones, page 28 *top right*: photograph by Anthony Jones from *Welsh Chapels*, Alan Sutton, 1996.

BBC, page 28 *bottom*.

The National Portrait Gallery, page 37 *left*.

Manchester City Art Galleries, page 37 *right*.

Introduction

This study guide is for you to use, together with others, while reading two stories from a collection of short stories by Thomas Hardy called *Wessex Tales*. The stories were written about a hundred years ago when Thomas Hardy was famous for the many novels he had written. His novels and stories continue to be popular now and are often adapted for the screen. As you read, think about and discuss these stories, you will be able to consider why Hardy's writing has remained popular and what it has to say to us at the beginning of the twenty-first century.

This guide contains:

- activities to help you to understand how Thomas Hardy came to write these stories

- background information to help you to put yourself into the world Hardy describes

- story-poems by Hardy and by Rudyard Kipling to help you to explore situations similar to those in the stories

- suggested ways to read and present the poems

- activities before you start reading to help you to focus on some of the ideas Hardy presents to you

- ideas to consider and discuss during your reading of the stories

- activities that encourage you to look more closely at the way Hardy builds and writes his stories

- a range of assignments for you to choose from to show what you have learnt from your experience of reading the stories

- extension activities to encourage you to explore more of Hardy's writing.

Thomas Hardy

Thomas Hardy was born in 1840 and died when he was nearly 90 in 1928. Here are two photographs of him – one taken when he was 16, the other when he was near the end of his life.

Thomas Hardy,
aged 16 and aged 81

Hardy spent his childhood in a small village near the edge of the wild moorland that he called Egdon Heath in his stories, and many miles from the nearest town.

This is how he described the family's cottage in one of his earliest poems:

> Our house stood quite alone, and those tall firs
> And beeches were not planted. Snakes and efts   efts: lizards
> Swarmed in the summer days, and nightly bats
> Would fly about our bedrooms. Heathcroppers   Heathcroppers: wild ponies
> Lived on the hills, and were our only friends;
> So wild it was when first we settled there.

He walked long distances to visit his relatives in Puddletown and to travel any further he would have used the carrier's cart or ridden on horseback. When the sun set in the evening, his cottage would have been lit by tallow candles and firelight, and without streetlamps the neighbouring heath would have been pitch dark and menacing to a child. Like most country children, Hardy spent the long evenings near the fire listening to his grandmother and his parents telling stories about the past and about the neighbourhood they had lived in for generations. As he grew up, the people he knew and listened to worked on the land. They had hard lives, but they understood and respected the countryside and the weather, and carried on traditions that had lasted for centuries. They lived in close communities and often met together for enjoyment … like the dances where Hardy's father played dance tunes on his violin. The nearest town, Dorchester (or Casterbridge in Hardy's stories), was only five miles away from his village, but a long distance to travel on foot or by cart. Hardy would have seen the town in the distance from Rushy Pond at the edge of the heath, as he did once through his father's telescope when he saw, magnified through the lens, an execution taking place on the roof of Dorchester gaol.

By yourself or in a pair

Now that you have some idea of the background of Hardy's life as a child in the first half of the nineteenth century, look back at the photographs of him as a young and old man, then make a list together of the changes and events you think he will have lived through during the rest of his life until his death in 1928.

When he was older, Hardy experienced life in London and other big cities. He owned cars and lived in a modern house in Dorchester with a telephone and electricity. Recorded music and dance bands had begun to replace musicians playing country dances. An efficient railway system linked people with the outside world and brought modern ways of life into the countryside. Yet, when Hardy began to write his stories as novels, short stories and poems, he chose to set most of them in the past, during the first years of the nineteenth century when his grandparents and parents were young and before he himself was born. The two *Wessex Tales* you are going to read are both set at a time ten to fifteen years before Hardy's birth.

Although he knew London and London people well, the characters he chose to create in his stories were mostly people whose families had lived for generations in the small area of Dorset that he knew best.

In a pair

Hardy decided to set his stories:

- in a past he knew about only from his childhood experiences and from listening to the memories of older people

- in the small country area he had lived in as a child.

If you had been able to interview Hardy, and ask him why he had made his decision, what reasons do you think he might have given you?

Together, make a list of those reasons.

In the introduction to one of his novels, Hardy explained one of his reasons. He wrote that he hoped to 'preserve for my own satisfaction a fairly true record of a vanishing life'. Were any of the reasons your group suggested similar to Hardy's?

The Wessex of Hardy's Wessex Tales

In the North of England, in Yorkshire, people arrive in coachloads to visit 'Heartbeat Country' and 'The Country of Last of the Summer Wine'. In Derbyshire, they visit 'Peak Practice Country' and, in Northern Ireland, 'Ballykissangel Country'.

Many writers, of television series and of printed stories, choose to set them in places they know well. Some describe and name those places so accurately that readers can visit streets and look for buildings that have become familiar to them through the stories they've read. The novelist James Joyce set his stories in Dublin and they are so precisely located that readers could trace the journeys of the characters on a real street map of the city. Other writers choose to create new worlds for their stories that could never be found in a real set of maps. J.R. Tolkien created Middle Earth for novels like The Hobbit and included his own made-up maps for readers to follow the action of the stories.

Thomas Hardy created Wessex, and his novels and short stories, like Wessex Tales, are printed with a copy of his made-up map so that readers can follow the action if they wish to. Unlike Tolkien's Middle Earth, but like 'Heartbeat Country' or Ballykissangel, Wessex is based on a real world, an area in the South West of England that, in real life, includes counties like Dorset, Somerset, Oxfordshire and Devon. Here is a copy of Hardy's original map.

The centre of that world is based on the small area of Dorset near Dorchester, where Hardy grew up. But, unlike the action of James Joyce's stories, the action of Hardy's novels and short stories cannot be traced on an actual map. You could not find the real Dorchester on a map of Wessex, but you could find Casterbridge sited where Dorchester should be. Hardy used the location of places he knew but gave them new names. He called

Map of Wessex

the whole 'world' Wessex because that part of the South West had been the site of Wessex, the ancient kingdom of the Angles and Saxons in Britain. You might have come across other areas in Britain that have two identities in a similar way. Nottinghamshire is real, but it is also the 'Robin Hood Country' of legends, books and films. Tintagel in Cornwall is real, but for many people it is the castle of King Arthur, the Camelot of legends, books and films.

As Hardy's stories are set in the near-past and in a half-made-up world, it is not surprising that Hardy himself described Wessex as 'real', but also 'half dream'. The creation of Wessex gave him the opportunity to comment on the world he knew, but also the freedom to use his imagination and not to be tied down by facts.

By yourself or in a pair

The two stories you are going to read and think about are set in the area of Wessex near to Casterbridge.

In 'The Withered Arm', the action takes place around the village of Holmstoke, which is midway between Anglebury and Casterbridge, in the valley of the River Froom and near the southern edge of Egdon Heath. In the story, the main characters take fateful journeys into Egdon Heath and across the Heath to Casterbridge. The main male character, Farmer Lodge, leaves the area at the end of the story and settles in Port Bredy.

Map of Dorchester area and place names

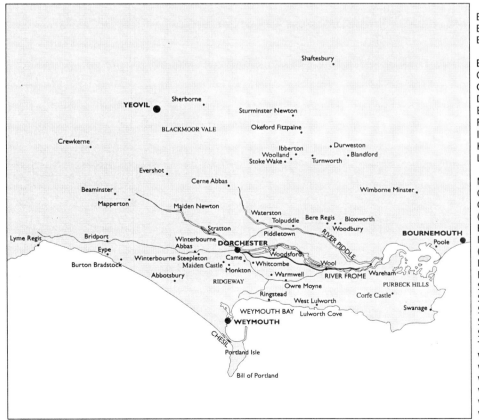

Real names	Fictional names
Abbotsbury	Abbotsea
Athelhampton	Athelhall
Bere Regis	Kingsbere and King's Bere
Bill of Portland	The Beal
Bockhampton	Mellstock
Blandford	Shottsford and Shottsford Forum
Bridport	Port Bredy
Cerne Abbas	Abbot's-Cernel
Corfe Castle	Corvesgate Castle
Dorchester	Casterbridge
Evershot	Evershead
Fordington	Durnover
Isle of Portland	Isle of Slingers
Kingston Maurward	Knapwater House
Lulworth Cove	Lulstead or Lulwind Cove
Maiden Newton	Chalk Newton
Oakford Fitzpaine	Oakbury Fitzpiers
Owre Moyne (Owermoigne)	Nether Moynton
Poole	Havenpool
Piddletown (Puddletown)	Weatherbury
Rainbarrows	Rainbarrow
Ringstead	Ringsworth
Sherborne	Sherton Abbas
Shaftesbury	Shaston
Stinsford	Mellstock
Swanage	Knollsea
Sturminster Newton	Stourcastle
Tolpuddle	Tolchurch
Wareham	Anglebury
Warmwell Cross	Warm'ell Cross
Wimborne	Warborne
Weymouth	Budmouth
Woodbury Hill	Greenhill
Wool	Wellbridge

In 'The Distracted Preacher', the action takes place in Nether Moynton, a few miles inland from the coast. The preacher follows Lizzy, the woman he loves, to dangerous meetings on the cliffs at Ringsworth and Lulwind Cove. One important moment in the story takes place at Warm'ell Cross.

Using the geographical map of the Dorchester area in Dorset and the list of Wessex names Hardy gave to real places, find the locations for the events in the two stories.

Tales

In the days before televisions and films and in the country where many couldn't read, people still loved stories. Instead of seeing or reading them, they heard them; people told each other stories. Sometimes these stories were re-told memories, at other times they were folk tales, legends passed on by story-tellers for centuries. Thomas Hardy's childhood was filled with story-telling – from his grandmother, who lived with the family, and from both his parents. This is an extract from Hardy's poem 'One we Knew', about how he and his sister used to sit by the fire listening to their grandmother telling tales.

> She showed us the spot where the maypole was yearly planted,
> And where the bandsmen stood
> While breeched and kerchiefed partners whirled, and panted
> To choose one another for good –
>
> She told us of the far-back day when they learnt astounded
> Of the death of the King of France;
> Of the Terror; and then of Bonaparte's unbounded
> Ambition and arrogance –
>
> She said she often heard the gibbet creaking
> As it swayed in the lightning flash,
> Had caught from the neighbouring town a small child's shrieking
> At the cart under the lash –
>
> With cap-framed face and long gaze into the embers –
> We seated around her knees –
> She would dwell on such dead themes, not as one remembers,
> But rather as one who sees.

From his grandmother, he heard about the history of their cottage, how she remembered it as a 'safe house' for smugglers bringing barrels of contraband brandy inland from the coast. From his father, he heard about one of his workmates who had been a smuggler and had carried heavy barrels strapped to his shoulders in his cross-country flight from the customs officers. His father also told him stories of the hardships of farm workers at the beginning of the century and of straw ricks that were burnt in angry demonstrations against wealthy farmers and landowners. Hardy heard of harsh punishments and gruesome executions. His mother was the teller of tales of superstition and 'magic'. Hardy listened to her accounts of strange cures, like 'turning the blood' by touching a convict's corpse, and mysterious tales of the supernatural, like the story of the woman, who, on a hot afternoon was visited by a powerful spirit or incubus which pressed down on her as she dozed.

When Hardy collected together several short stories set in Wessex, he gave them the title *Wessex Tales* because they are all based in different ways on tales he heard or heard about from Dorset people. He was putting onto paper his version of the folk tales he had heard, for people who lived far from Dorset to read.

In a pair

Look again at the poem on page 6. Discuss what you think Hardy meant by the last two lines of the poem.

Take it in turns to tell each other tales you've heard from older people, maybe from your grandparents or parents. At the end of this study guide, there will be an opportunity to follow Hardy's example and to write your version of some of these tales.

Before reading
the story

Here is a group of Hardy's poems that – like the story you are going to read, 'The Withered Arm' – tell about relationships between men and women.

Read these through on your own and try to record:

* your thoughts and feelings

* questions you would like to ask someone else

* your comments on lines and phrases that you like.

A Trampwoman's Tragedy

From Wynyard's Gap the livelong day,
   The livelong day,
We beat afoot the northward way
   We had travelled times before.
The sun-blaze burning on our backs,
Our shoulders sticking to our packs,
By fosseway, fields, and turnpike tracks
   We skirted sad Sedge-Moor.

Full twenty miles we jaunted on.
   We jaunted on, –
My fancy-man, and jeering John,
   And Mother Lee, and I.
And, as the sun drew down to west,
We climbed the toilsome Poldon crest,
And saw, of landskip sights the best,
   The inn that beamed thereby.

For months we had padded side by side,
   Ay, side by side
Through the Great Forest, Blackmoor wide,
   And where the Parret ran.
We'd faced the gusts on Mendip ridge,
Had crossed the Yeo unhelped by bridge,
Been stung by every Marshwood midge,
   I and my fancy-man.

Lone inns we loved, my man and I,
   My man and I;
'King's Stag', 'Windwhistle' high and dry,
   'The Horse' on Hintock Green,
The cosy house at Wynyard's Gap,
'The Hut' renowned on Bredy Knap,
And many another wayside tap
   Where folk might sit unseen.

Now as we trudged – O deadly day,
    O deadly day! –
I teased my fancy man in play
    And wanton idleness.
I walked alongside jeering John,
I laid his hand my waist upon;
I would not bend my glances on
    My lover's dark distress.

Thus Poldon top at last we won,
    At last we won,
And gained the inn at sink of sun
    Far-famed as 'Marshall's Elm'.
Beneath us figured tor and lea,
From Mendip to the western sea –
I doubt if finer sight there be
    Within this royal realm.

Inside the settle all a-row –
    All four a-row
We sat, I next to John, to show
    That he had wooed and won.
And then he took me on his knee,
And swore it was his turn to be
My favoured mate, and Mother Lee
    Passed to my former one.

Then in a voice I had never heard,
    I had never heard,
My only Love to me: 'One word,
    My lady, if you please!
Whose is the child you are like to bear? –
His? After all my months o' care?'
God knows 'twas not! But, O despair!
    I nodded – still to tease.

Then up he sprung, and with his knife –
    And with his knife
He let out jeering Johnny's life,
    Yes; there, at set of sun.
The slant ray through the window nigh
Gilded John's blood and glazing eye,
Ere scarcely Mother Lee and I
    Knew that the deed was done.

The taverns tell the gloomy tale,
    The gloomy tale,
How that at Ivel-chester jail
    My Love, my sweetheart swung;
Though stained till now by no misdeed
Save one horse ta'en in time o' need;
(Blue Jimmy stole right many a steed
    Ere his last fling he flung.)

Thereaft I walked the world alone,
    Alone, alone!
On his death-day I gave my groan
    And dropt his dead-born child.
'Twas nigh the jail, beneath a tree,
None tending me; for Mother Lee
Had died at Glaston, leaving me
    Unfriended on the wild.

And in the night as I lay weak,
    As I lay weak,
The leaves a-falling on my cheek,
    The red moon low declined –
The ghost of him I'd die to kiss
Rose up and said: 'Ah, tell me this!
Was the child mine, or was it his?
    Speak, that I rest may find!'

O doubt not but I told him then,
    I told him then,
That I had kept me from all men
    Since we joined lips and swore.
Whereat he smiled, and thinned away
As the wind stirred to call up day ...
– 'Tis past! And here alone I stray
    Haunting the Western Moor.

Faintheart in a Railway Train

At nine in the morning there passed a church,
At ten there passed me by the sea,
At twelve a town of smoke and smirch,
At two a forest of oak and birch,
    And, then, on a platform, she:

A radiant stranger, who saw not me.
I said, 'Get out to her do I dare?'
But I kept my seat in my search for a plea,
And the wheels moved on. O could it but be
    That I had alighted there!

A Hurried Meeting

It is August moonlight in the tall plantation,
Whose elms, by aged squirrels' footsteps worn,
   Outscreen the noon, and eve, and morn.
On the facing slope a faint irradiation
   From a mansion's marble front is borne,
     Mute in its woodland wreathing.
     Up here the night-jar whirrs forlorn,
And the trees seem to withold their softest breathing.

To the moonshade slips a woman in muslin vesture:
Her naked neck the gossamer-web besmears
   And she sweeps it away with a hasty gesture.
Again it touches her forehead, her neck, her ears,
     Her fingers, the backs of her hands.
     She sweeps it away again
     Impatiently, and then
She takes no notice; and listens, and sighs, and stands.

The night-hawk stops. A man shows in the obscure:
     They meet, and passively kiss,
And he says: 'Well, I've come quickly. About this –
     Is it really so? You are sure?'
    'I am sure. In February it will be.
   That such a thing should come to me!
We should have known. We should have left off meeting.
Love is a terrible thing: a sweet allure
     That ends in heart-outeating!'

  'But what shall we do, my Love, and how?'
  'You need not call me by that name now.'
Then he more coldly: 'What is your suggestion?'
'I've told my mother, and she sees a way,
Since of our marriage there can be no question.
We are crossing South – near about New Year's Day
     The event will happen there.
It is the only thing that we can dare
     To keep them unaware!'
     'Well, you can marry me.'
She shook her head. 'No, that can never be.

''Twill be brought home as hers. She's forty-one,
When many a woman's bearing is not done,
     And well might have a son. –
We should have left off specious self-deceiving:
     I feared that such might come,
     And knowledge struck me numb.
Love is a terrible thing: witching when first begun,
     To end in grieving, grieving!'

And with one kiss again the couple parted:
Inferior clearly he; she haughty-hearted.
He watched her down the slope to return to her place,
The marble mansion of her ancient race,
And saw her brush the gossamers from her face
As she emerged from shade to moonlight ray.
    And when she had gone away
  The night-jar seemed to imp, and say,
    'You should have taken warning:
Love is a terrible thing: sweet for a space,
    And then all mourning, mourning!'

We Sat at the Window

We sat at the window looking out,
And the rain came down like silken strings
That Swithin's day. Each gutter and spout
Babbled unchecked in the busy way
    Of witless things:
Nothing to read, nothing to see
Seemed in that room for her and me
    On Swithin's day.

We were irked by the scene, by our own selves; yes,
For I did not know, nor did she infer
How much there was to read and guess
By her in me, and to see and crown
    By me in her.
Wasted were two souls in their prime,
And great was the waste, that July time
    When the rain came down.

At Tea

The kettle descants in a cosy drone,
And the young wife looks in her husband's face,
And then at her guest's, and shows in her own
Her sense that she fills an envied place;
And the visiting lady is all abloom,
And says there was never so sweet a room.

And the happy young housewife does not know
That the woman beside her was first his choice,
Till the fates ordained it could not be so...
Betraying nothing in look or voice
The guest sits smiling and sips her tea,
And he throws her a stray glance yearningly.

Under the Waterfall

'Whenever I plunge my arm, like this,
In a basin of water, I never miss
The sweet sharp sense of a fugitive day
Fetched back from its thickening shroud of gray.
      Hence the only prime
      And real love-rhyme
      That I know by heart,
      And that leaves no smart,
Is the purl of a little valley fall
About three spans wide and two spans tall
Over a table of solid rock,
And into a scoop of the self-same block;
The purl of a runlet that never ceases
In stir of kingdoms, in wars, in peaces;
With a hollow boiling voice it speaks
And has spoken since hills were turfless peaks.'

'And why gives this the only prime
Idea to you of a real love-rhyme?
And why does plunging your arm in a bowl
Full of spring water, bring throbs to your soul?'

'Well, under the fall, in a crease of the stone,
Though where precisely none ever has known,
Jammed darkly, nothing to show how prized,
And by now with its smoothness opalized,
      Is a drinking-glass:
      For, down that pass
      My lover and I
      Walked under a sky
Of blue with a leaf-wove awning of green,
In the burn of August, to paint the scene,
And we placed our basket of fruit and wine
By the runlet's rim, where we sat to dine;
And when we had drunk from the glass together,
Arched by the oak-copse from the weather,
I held the vessel to rinse in the fall,
Where it slipped, and sank, and was past recall,
Though we stooped and plumbed the little abyss
With long bared arms. There the glass still is.
And, as I said, if I thrust my arm below
Cold water in basin or bowl, a throe
From the past awakens a sense of that time,
And the glass we used, and the cascade's rhyme.
The basin seems the pool, and its edge
The hard smooth face of the brook-side ledge,
And the leafy pattern of china-ware
The hanging plants that were bathing there.

'By night, by day, when it shines or lours,
There lies intact that chalice of ours,
And its presence adds to the rhyme of love
Persistently sung by the fall above.
No lip has touched it since his and mine
In turns therefrom sipped lovers' wine.'

In a group of four

1   Talk together about the poems you've read. Take each poem in turn and use your notes to ask each other questions and to tell each other how you felt about the relationship pictured in each poem. When you've talked about each of the poems, discuss your overall impressions. Would you call these poems love stories?

2   Choose four poems for reading in a taped poetry programme or for presenting in a display.

3   When you've made your choices, make sure through discussion that you understand each of the chosen poems. Decide:
    * *either*, in what tone of voice each should be read
    * *or*, what kind of illustration should be found or drawn to suggest the mood of each.

4   Write a short paragraph to introduce each poem, and a conclusion to your whole presentation to explain what you've noticed about Thomas Hardy's picture of relationships between men and women.

5   Finally:
    * *either* record your programme on tape for others to hear
    * *or* present a display of the poems with your accompanying illustrations and commentaries.

Discussion activities for groups

Activity 1

Several of the *Wessex Tales*, including 'The Withered Arm', show how in the early nineteenth century people who broke the law were severely punished. Some were executed for crimes we would think of as minor offences. Hardy's strong feelings about such punishments began in his childhood when he heard about the hanging of four young men whose only crime was to be at the scene when a hay rick was set on fire.

By yourself

To prepare to discuss your feelings about capital punishment:

* look at the drawing of a public hanging that took place in the early years of the nineteenth century

* read the fact sheet about capital punishment in the eighteenth, nineteenth and twentieth centuries.

A public hanging, *c.* 1800

Capital punishment	
Date	**Facts**
18th and early 19th century	Over 200 offences carried the penalty of capital punishment. These included petty theft and forgery. Executions were usually carried out in public and drew large crowds of observers. Hardy himself witnessed at least two.
1823	The death penalty was abolished for over a hundred crimes in Britain.
1825	In Dorset, executions were carried out as punishment for horse-stealing, burglary and arson.
1868	After recommendations from the 1865 Royal Commission, public execution was abolished and capital punishment carried out in prisons.
1956	A Bill to abolish the death penalty was passed by the Commons but defeated by the Lords.
1957	Capital punishment was retained only for certain kinds of murder, for example, murder in resisting arrest or murder committed in the course or furtherance of theft.
1965	The death penalty was abolished for all forms of murder.
1979	In parliament, a motion for the re-introduction of capital punishment was defeated in a free vote by a majority of 119.

There have been many methods of execution – the guillotine in France; the firing squad; hanging; and the gas chamber, lethal injection and the electric chair in the USA.

In the USA, some states retain the death penalty. Prisoners can be kept in uncertainty on 'Death Row' for many years while their fates are decided.

In a group of four

Take it in turns to explain to the others how you feel about capital punishment. You will be able to use the fact sheet to support the views you express. When each of you has had a turn, discuss the views you have heard.

Activity 2

In the country areas of Dorset where Hardy grew up, people believed strongly in witchcraft and superstitions. To protect themselves against witches they wore bags of charms next to their skin and planted rowan trees next to their houses. If they cut their skin with a knife they buried the knife in damp ground, believing that as the blade rusted their cut would heal. If they wanted to know the future or heal a mysterious illness they would consult wise men and women like Conjuror Trendle, who plays an important part in 'The Withered Arm'. Hardy based this story on two tales he had heard in his youth, one about witchcraft and one about a mysterious healing. Before you read the story, think about your own attitude to superstitions and alternative forms of healing.

In pairs

1   Make two lists together of any examples you know of:
    *   superstitions
    *   alternative forms of medicine.

2   Discuss these questions.
    *   Do you believe in any of the superstitions on your list? Why?
    *   Do you believe that any of the alternative forms of medicine are successful? Why?

By yourself

Thinking about the title and about the activities on the previous pages, what sort of story do you think 'The Withered Arm' will be? What sorts of character and action do you expect?

Reading the story   During your reading of the story, break off to think, talk and write about what you've felt and thought.

Talk in pairs or jot down by yourself responses to these questions.

Parts 1 and 2

1   In the first two pages, we find out that Rhoda Brook milks her cows 'somewhat apart from the rest' and her house is in 'a lonely spot' away from the village. What do you think Hardy is suggesting to us at the beginning of the story, about her character, her relationship with the villagers and her past life?

2   At first sight, it seems that Hardy doesn't tell us much about Rhoda's son – but look again at Parts 1 and 2. Can you discover any clues to his character?

3   How do you feel when Rhoda sends her son to find out about Farmer Lodge's new wife?

4 As Hardy doesn't describe Farmer Lodge's feelings – before and after passing the boy in the road, imagine what they would have been and then jot down or discuss your ideas. Remember who the boy is and that Farmer Lodge is driving his new wife home in a fashionable lemon and red-coloured gig, while the boy is struggling to walk with a heavy bundle.

5 Look back to find out what Rhoda and Gertrude look and dress like. What are the chief differences between them? You may be helped by these photographs, taken in the nineteenth century, of a milkmaid and of a young woman in church.

6 At the end of Part 2, Rhoda has an image of Mrs Lodge in her mind that is as 'realistic as a photograph'. Photographs were a new invention when Hardy wrote this story. What do you think he wants to make the reader realise?

7 At this stage, do you think your predictions of the story will prove to be right?

Parts 3, 4 and 5

1 At the end of Part 3, Rhoda wonders whether she has witch-like powers and whether this could be the explanation for her nightmarish experience and the link with the marks on Gertrude's arm. Re-read carefully the description of her experience at the beginning of Part 3. Do you think this was a supernatural happening? Or can you suggest a rational explanation? It might help to remind yourselves of your

response to the sixth question set on Parts 1 and 2.

2 For two or three weeks, Rhoda knows about Gertrude only from descriptions, but after their first meeting she sees her several times during Parts 3 and 4. What changes did you see developing in her attitude to the young woman? How far do you sympathise with Rhoda at this point in the story?

3 As Gertrude's arm grew more withered, more and more people in the neighbourhood would have known about it. Jot down or talk about the reactions of these different people: Gertrude herself, Farmer Lodge, the villagers, Rhoda.

4 The villagers call Conjuror Trendle an 'exorcist' or magician. When you meet him in the story, does he match up to your image of a traditional magician? Do you think he does have special powers? What is your evidence?

5 We don't read about Gertrude's thoughts and feelings as she leaves Conjuror Trendle's house, we see only that 'her face was so rigid as to wear an oldened aspect'. What has happened to change her? What do you think she now realises and feels about Rhoda – and about her husband?

6 Why do you think Rhoda and her son left Holmstoke?

Parts 6 and 7

1 Hardy describes the Lodges' six-year marriage as sunk 'into prosiness, and worse'. Re-read the beginning of Part 6, as far as Gertrude's words, 'If I could only again be as I was when he first saw me!'. What do you now understand by Hardy's description?

2 Now that you've read again about the Lodges' marriage, by yourself or together, make two lists of reasons for feeling sympathy for:
• Farmer Lodge
• Gertrude.

For which of the two do you feel more sympathy?

3 When Gertrude's arm was first affected, she was reluctant to consult Conjuror Trendle. Now, she's prepared to travel fifteen miles to Casterbridge by herself to carry out Conjuror Trendle's suggested cure. What does this tell you about the state of her feelings at this point in the story, and about the changes that have taken place in her character?

4 Whose side of the story did you see in the first five parts of the story? Whose side are you seeing now? Does this change make you feel any differently about the main characters in the story?

Parts 8 and 9

1 Gertrude faces many problems when she decides to follow Conjuror Trendle's suggested cure for her arm. By yourself or together, make a list of these problems and, for each one, discover how she overcomes it. What do you think was the worst problem for her? Why?

2 Like Conjuror Trendle, the hangman lives in a 'lonely cottage' and Gertrude is nervous about visiting him. When you meet him in Part 8, does he seem an alarming person?

3 Look back to the hangman's description of the young man who is to be hanged and find out about his crime. How does the hangman feel about him? Now look at the moment near the end of Part 8 when Gertrude asks, 'Where is it now?' and the hangman replies, 'It? – he, you mean; he's living yet'. Five years before, Gertrude had been kind to poor villagers like Rhoda's son. Has she lost her kindness now?

4 What were your reactions to the climax of the story in the final part, when the identity of the corpse was revealed? Had you guessed who it might be? Had there been any clues that prepared – or might have prepared – you for the discovery?

5 When Rhoda sees Gertrude she cries, 'Hussy – to come between us and our child now!'. At that moment in the story, where do your sympathies lie? With Gertrude? With Farmer Lodge? With Rhoda? With Rhoda and Lodge's son? Why?

6 The story closes with three of the main characters dead, at a young age. What or whom do you blame for their deaths?

After reading the story

The activities in this section give you the opportunity to express your feelings and thoughts now that you've finished reading the story.

Working with others: talking

Activity 1

In a group of four, look back together at the poems by Hardy you read before 'The Withered Arm'. Discuss whether you can see any links between the stories they tell about relationships between men and women, and the story of Rhoda, Gertrude and Farmer Lodge.

Activity 2

1 To prepare for your discussion, by yourself, look back:
   - at the hangman's explanation of the boy's crime in Part 8
   - at the descriptions of the crowd in the harness shop in Part 7
   - at the description of the hanged boy's body and the effects of the execution on his parents.

2   In the same group as for the discussion of capital punishment before reading the story (page 15), discuss whether reading 'The Withered Arm' has had any effect on your previous feelings and thoughts about capital punishment.

Activity 3

In a group of three or four, read the statement by one of the first readers of 'The Withered Arm', Leslie Stephen, and the reply written by Hardy:

> [If I were writing the story], I would accept the superstition altogether and make the wizard a genuine performer … or I would leave some opening as to the withering of the arm, so that a possibility of explanation might be suggested.
>
> *(Leslie Stephen)*

> … a story dealing with the supernatural should never be explained away.
>
> *(Thomas Hardy)*

With these views in your minds discuss:

* 'The Withered Arm'

* 'supernatural' stories you've read or seen.

Do you agree with Leslie Stephen that the withered arm should either have been clearly the result of witchcraft, or clearly the result of an explained happening? Or do you agree with Hardy that nothing should have been clearly explained?

Talking and acting

Activity 1

* In a group of five or six, prepare to 'hot-seat' Farmer Lodge and Rhoda about the deaths of Gertrude and the son.

* Those playing the parts should prepare their defences, and the rest of the group should prepare questions to ask them.

* Act out the 'hot-seating', either on tape or for the rest of the class.

Activity 2

In a group of three

Hardy does not include in his story the scene when Rhoda contacted Farmer Lodge, for the first time for many years, to tell him about the arrest and trial of their son and his sentence of execution. We don't know where they met – it might have been Casterbridge, or in a lonely place they both knew, perhaps by the pond at the edge of Egdon Heath, but they will certainly have met in secret. We don't know where Rhoda and her son have been living since they left Holmstoke, but they will certainly have led a hard life. We do know, from evidence near the beginning of Part 7, that their meeting must have taken place in the summer between haymaking and harvest, and that Farmer Lodge has told Gertrude a lie about taking a holiday without her in order to explain his absence from home.

Prepare to improvise or to tape the scene of their meeting. Decide who is to play each of the parts and which of you is to be the director of the acted scene, or technician in charge of sound effects for the tape.

As an important part of preparing to act, or write the script for taping, you will need to discuss:

- the feelings each of the characters brings to the meeting

- the information each one will want to give the other

- the aspects of the past they will talk about and the questions they will ask each other

- the plans they will make to meet in Casterbridge for the execution

- how their feelings for and about each other will develop during the meeting

- how they will talk about their son and what has happened to him.

Either: improvise and work on the scene with the aim of showing it to the rest of the group.

Or: write the script for taping (with sound effects and possibly a part for a narrator), rehearse and tape.

Working by yourself: writing
Activity 1 – looking at the way Hardy writes

Read the following extract from Part 1 of the story. The numbers link up with some points you'll be asked to comment on after you've finished reading.

Their course lay apart from that of the others, to a lonely spot high above the water-meads, and not far from the border of Egdon Heath, whose dark countenance was visible in the distance (1) as they drew nigh to their home.

'They've just been saying down in Barton that your father brings his young wife home from Anglebury to-morrow,' the woman observed. 'I shall want to send you for a few things to market, and you'll be pretty sure to meet 'em.'

'Yes, mother,' said the boy. 'Is father married then?'

'Yes ... You can give her a look, and tell me what she's like, if you do see her.' (2)

'Yes, mother.'

'If she's dark or fair, and if she's tall – as tall as I. And if she seems like a woman who has ever worked for a living, or one that has been always well off, and has never done anything, and shows marks of the lady on her, as I expect she do.'

'Yes.'

They crept up the hill in the twilight (3) and entered the cottage. It was built of mud-walls, the surface of which had been washed by many rains into channels and depressions that left none of the original flat face visible; while here and there in the thatch above a rafter showed like a bone protruding through the skin. (4)

She was kneeling down in the chimney-corner, before two pieces of turf laid together with the heather inwards, blowing at the red-hot ashes with her breath till the turves flamed. The radiance lit her pale cheek, and made her dark eyes, that had once been handsome, seem handsome anew. (5) 'Yes,' she resumed, ' see if she is dark or fair, and if you can, notice if her hands be white; if not, see if they look as though she had ever done housework, or are milker's hands like mine.'

The boy again promised, inattentively this time, his mother not observing that he was cutting a notch with his pocket-knife in the beech-backed chair. (6)

Write your answers to the following questions, as fully as you can.

1   Hardy describes Egdon Heath as having a 'dark countenance', or face, that is 'visible in the distance'. Remember the part Egdon Heath plays in the story. How does Hardy suggest its later atmosphere and importance in these words?

2   The dots near the beginning of Rhoda's words show that she is pausing to think and feel as she talks to her son. If you were asked to read out loud the sentence after the dots, explain, with your reasons, in what tone of voice you would read it to show Rhoda's thoughts and feelings. For example, would she speak enthusiastically? or angrily? or in an offhand, careless way?

3   Why do you think Hardy chose the words 'crept up' to describe the movements of Rhoda and her son, instead of 'walked up' or 'climbed'?

4   Read the whole description of the outside of the cottage. What is Hardy suggesting to you through this description about the lives of Rhoda and her son? Look particularly at the simile (or comparison) 'in the thatch above a rafter showed like a bone protruding through the skin'.

5   As night was falling, it would have been important for Rhoda to re-start the fire as soon as she entered the cottage. Hardy uses her actions, though, to help readers to form a picture in their minds. What is the picture?

6   This sentence can tell you several things about the boy and his relationships with his mother and father. Which words do you think are the most important in the sentence? Why?

Look carefully at this illustration from a modern edition of 'The Withered Arm'. It appears just before the passage you have been considering.

Jot down your answers to these questions.

- What's being shown in the illustration? Who are the two figures on the left?

- Why do you think the illustrator has placed these two figures right at the edge of the drawing?

- What is the dark area behind the buildings? What effect does it have on the picture?

- Do you think the illustration adds anything to Hardy's words at this point in the story? Does it help you to understand? to picture characters or scenes more clearly? to sense the atmosphere more vividly?

Activity 2

After the deaths of his son and his wife, Farmer Lodge lived on, alone, for two years. During the story, Hardy gives us few clues to his feelings and reactions.

- Re-read the story and make notes of any clues you can find.

- Then imagine that he has decided to put his side of the story, perhaps in talking to a sympathetic listener. Write down his version of the events told in 'The Withered Arm'.

Activity 3

Write two articles for two front pages of the Casterbridge newspaper for the year 1825, including appropriate headlines. If you want to set the page out like a newspaper, you can find evidence in the story of the kind of news and advertisements that might have appeared.

- Article 1 – announcing the public execution of the boy, and including an account of his crime. Remember that the story tells us how fascinated people were in hangings.

- Article 2 – an account of the sensational happenings in the gaol on the day of the hanging. Include extracts from interviews with the hangman, the inn keeper who served Gertrude, and with people from Holmstoke who knew the Lodges and Rhoda.

Activity 4

Write your account of the effects that Farmer Lodge had on the lives and characters of (a) Rhoda and (b) Gertrude. You will need to go back to the story first to find and make notes of your evidence. As a conclusion, explain how you feel about the triangular relationship between these three people, and about what the story shows you about the choices men and women had in the time when the story was set.

Activity 5

Write in-depth interviews with (a) Conjuror Trendle and (b) the hangman about their ways of life, the places they lived in, their impressions of Rhoda and Gertrude and of the withered arm. You will need to re-read the relevant parts of the story to find your evidence and make notes of the information you'll use.

At the centre of the story 'The Distracted Preacher' is a village near the Wessex coast in which everyone is involved in some way in the smuggling of brandy from France. Rudyard Kipling's poem, 'A Smuggler's Song', will introduce you to some of the excitements and dangers that smuggling used to bring to small communities.

Read the poem to yourself.

A Smuggler's Song

If you wake at midnight, and hear a horse's feet,
Don't go drawing back the blind, or looking in the street,
Them that asks no questions isn't told a lie.
Watch the wall, my darling, while the Gentlemen go by!
    Five and twenty ponies,
    Trotting through the dark –
    Brandy for the Parson,
    'Baccy for the Clerk;
    Laces for a lady; letters for a spy,
    And watch the wall, my darling, while the Gentlemen go by!

Running round the woodlump if you chance to find
Little barrels, roped and tarred, all full of brandy-wine;
Don't you shout to come and look, nor take 'em for your play;
Put the brishwood back again, – and they'll be gone next day!

If you see the stableyard setting open wide;
If you see a tired horse lying down inside;
If your mother mends a coat cut about and tore;
If the lining's wet and warm – don't you ask no more!

If you meet King George's men, dressed in blue and red,
You be careful what you say, and mindful what is said.
If they call you 'pretty maid,' and chuck you 'neath the chin,
Don't you tell where no one is, nor yet where no one's been!

Knocks and footsteps round the house – whistles after dark –
You've no call for running out till the house-dogs bark.
Trusty's here, and Pincher's here, and see how dumb they lie –
They don't fret to follow when the Gentlemen go by!

If you do as you've been told, 'likely there's a chance,
You'll be given a dainty doll, all the way from France,
With a cap of Valenciennes, and a velvet hood –
A present from the Gentlemen, along o' being good!

Five and twenty ponies,
Trotting through the dark –
Brandy for the Parson,
'Baccy for the Clerk.

Them that asks no questions isn't told a lie –
Watch the wall, my darling, while the Gentlemen go by!

(Rudyard Kipling)

Ask yourself these questions about the poem and jot down your responses:

- Who do you think is the narrator of the poem? And who is 'my darling', the listener? There are several clues in the poem.

- 'Watch the wall, my darling, while the Gentlemen go by!' During the poem, what advice does the narrator give 'my darling' about how to react to the Gentlemen? How do other people in the village react to them?

- These days, smugglers (who bring into a country illegal goods like arms supplies or drugs, or goods on which they haven't paid custom duties) are treated as criminals and punished, often severely. Does this poem make the smugglers, the 'Gentlemen', seem like criminals? And how does it make you feel about the representatives of the law, 'King George's men'? What's the evidence you used for your answer?

In a group of three or four, prepare for a poetry video of 'A Smuggler's Song'. In a poetry video, visual images are seen on the screen to illustrate or suggest the different stages in a poem while voices read the poem on the soundtrack. There might be sound effects or atmospheric music to accompany the words.

You'll need to follow these stages:

- Decide what kind of visual images would suit the poem. You could choose from filmed action with actors, cartoon sequences, or photographic stills.

- Divide the poem up into 'scenes' and discuss the visual images you'll have to accompany each 'scene'.

- Discuss how the poem should be read. For example, should the phrase 'Watch the wall, my darling, while the Gentlemen go by!' be read in a sinister tone of voice? or like a threat? or in a reassuring tone? In the verse beginning 'Knocks and footsteps ...', what do the dashes between words suggest for the reader?

- Discuss what else might appear on the soundtrack, for example, atmospheric music before the reader begins? or the sound of horses' hooves?

- Present your plans for the video in storyboard form. Here's a suggested way of starting.

Poem into film

Lines from poem

If you wake at midnight, and hear a

horse's feet,

Don't go drawing back the blind, or

looking in the street ...

Film sequence

Comments

The person who has been asleep is

being warned not to look out into

the street when the sound of

horses' hooves wakes people up.

Video

The viewer sees a child sitting up

in bed and listening carefully and

fearfully to the noises outside.

Audio

The sound of several horses

going past in the street, hooves

echoing on the cobbles.

How to use the 'Poem into film' sheet

In the 'Film sequence' box	sketch the picture to suit the lines you have copied out.
Under 'Comments'	explain what the lines are saying.
Under 'Video'	explain in words what the viewer sees.
Under 'Audio'	explain the sound effects and/or music which might accompany the lines.

Talking together

One of the main characters in the story 'The Distracted Preacher' is a young Methodist minister. Look at these pictures, of a village church and a village Methodist chapel, and read the information.

Stinsford Church in Dorset where Thomas Hardy and his family are buried

A Welsh chapel

Methodists

Methodists are Christians who broke away from the Church of England in the late eighteenth century. They are called non-conformists or dissenters because they disagree with some of the ways in which the traditional church worships God. In the 1830s, when the story takes place, there would have been a new Methodist chapel and an ancient church in most towns and villages.

Vicars and ministers

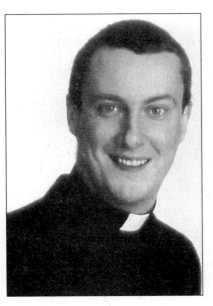

In Nether Moynton, the village in the story, the vicar who looked after the church had been there for many years. About half the people living in the village went to his Sunday morning services in the ancient church; the rest of the villagers went to the chapel. On Sunday evenings, most of the villagers went to the chapel service, to listen to the minister preaching.

Reverend Stockdale, the Methodist minister in the story, is young, unmarried and good-looking. He's lived in a town all his life but for his first job he's been sent at very short notice to Nether Moynton, a small village near the Wessex coast. He would be dressed rather like the priest in the photograph.

In a group of three or four, discuss the problems the new minister might meet in his first job. These might include problems:

- with living in a village community

- with the elderly vicar who's been in the village for many years

- with the young women in the village

- with the men who work on the land

- with the elderly people in the chapel congregation.

By yourself

Thinking about the title and about the previous activities, what sort of story do you think 'The Distracted Preacher' will be? What sort of characters and action do you expect? Jot down your predictions.

Look carefully at this modern illustration of part of 'The Distracted Preacher'. It appears at the beginning of the collection *Wessex Tales*, before readers have met the story.

Jot down your answers to the following questions about the illustration.

- What does the picture show you? Who do you think the people are?

- Look at the men's clothes and hats. How is the man on the right of the drawing different from the others? What do you think he might be doing?

- On the right-hand side of the church tower roof there are heads peeping out over the wall. Why do you think they might be there?

- As some of the men have long stakes in their hands and others seem to be digging in the churchyard, what do you guess they might be doing?

- How has the illustration added to the predictions you have already made?

Reading the story

During reading, break off to think, talk and write about what you've felt and thought.

Talk in pairs or jot down by yourself your responses to the following.

Part 1

- Remind yourselves of the description of Stockdale in the third paragraph. Imagine a group of villagers are talking about him soon after hearing his first sermon. What do you think the men – farmers and labourers – might say about him? What do you think the women might say?

- There are plenty of clues in Part 1 that tell you about Lizzy Newberry. Look back for them and jot down or talk together about your first impressions of her. For example, what does she look like? What does she think and feel about her new lodger? How is she treating him? The village boy said that Mrs Newberry's first husband had been a farmer. Have you discovered anything else about him?

- Did Stockdale realise all the things you've discovered about Lizzy? Jot down or talk together about his reactions to her – during his first few days as a lodger and when Lizzy takes him into the church. What difference does it make that he's a preacher?

Now that you've realised that you understand more about Lizzy and her life than Stockdale does, keep that in your mind as you carry on reading.

Parts 2 and 3

- 'She never had looked prettier, or more incomprehensible', 'the minister was in a cold sweat at the deception that she was practising', 'he lived on in perplexity'. These are phrases from Parts 2 and 3 that express Stockdale's confused feelings about Lizzy. Jot down by yourself or together make a list of the things that Stockdale doesn't understand. For example, why was the man watching from the laurel bush? What had Owlett come to say to Lizzy? Now, suggest an explanation for each of the things on your list.

- Remember that Stockdale is a minister at the beginning of his career. Why do you think he's so upset about the mysteries surrounding Lizzy?

- From the evidence of the story so far, do you think Stockdale and Lizzy would have a happy marriage?

Parts 4 and 5

- Look back at the list of mysteries you made after Parts 3 and 4. Were your guesses right? At what point did Stockdale realise the whole truth about Lizzy?

- In Part 4, Stockdale says angrily to Lizzy, 'You are in man's clothes and I am ashamed of you!'. These days, many women wear trousers, boots and long coats. Why is Stockdale so angry? Do you feel sympathy with him?

- The events of the night on the top of the cliff at Ringsworth in Part 4 and at Lulwind Cove in Part 5 were familiar for Lizzy, but new and strange for Stockdale. Jot down or talk together about (a) the thoughts and feelings of Lizzy on each of the nights, and (b) the thoughts and feelings of Stockdale on each of the nights. Don't forget that at the end of Part 4 Lizzy says, 'life would be so dull if it wasn't for that', and Stockdale says, 'all this is very wrong'.

- What are your predictions for the rest of the story? For example, will Latimer and his officers find the tubs of brandy? Will Lizzy give up the smuggling? Will Lizzy and Stockdale marry?

Parts 6 and 7

- How many of your predictions came true?

- The smugglers obviously had a well-prepared plan in case of being found out. From the evidence of the story, write the plan in the order that the villagers put it into operation.

- Look back at the way Latimer led the search for the smuggled brandy. His men did succeed in finding it. Does that mean that they were more clever and ingenious than the smugglers, or more dedicated, or luckier?

- Stockdale asked Lizzy to give up smuggling. Lizzy asked Stockdale to give up the ministry. They both refused. Do you think that means that they didn't love each other? Were they both stubborn? Or were there other reasons for their refusals? What would you have done if you had been Stockdale – or Lizzy?

- When Stockdale returned to Nether Moynton two years later, Lizzy described to him how Owlett was arrested. She explained how the officers had been given extra money, or 'blood money', for arresting smugglers, and how the officers had hunted them down 'like rats'. How do her words make you feel about the smugglers?

- Hardy wrote two endings for this story. When it was first published in a magazine, the story ended with the marriage of Lizzy and Stockdale, and their life as minister and wife in a town in the Midlands. Hardy himself would have preferred to end the story with the parting of Lizzy and Stockdale, and her emigration to America with the exiled Jim Owlett. Which ending do you prefer? Jot down or tell each other the reasons for your choice.

After reading the story

The activities in this section give you the opportunity to express your feelings and thoughts now that you've finished reading the story.

Working with others: dramatising

Activity 1

In a group of four

'The Distracted Preacher' would make a good radio play for voices and sound effects.

- Choose one sequence from the story that could be suspenseful, for example, the episode when Stockdale and Lizzy watch and listen to the smugglers above Lulwind Cove (the beginning of Part 5), or the episode when Stockdale goes back to find Latimer at Warm'ell Cross (Part 7).

- Choose one sequence that focuses on Stockdale and Lizzy, for example, their first meetings (Part 1), or their big argument (Part 7).

For each scene you choose, create your script in rough draft.

- Write the words for a narrator to introduce the scene with a few sentences of story-telling. They could be taken from the story itself.

- Decide how many characters will speak in the scene.

- Write down their dialogue. You will probably use the dialogue from the story, but you may decide to cut some of it out, and/or to add some that you write for yourselves. Set out the dialogue in the form of a play. To help the actors, add advice in brackets about how they should speak the lines, for example,

  > STOCKDALE (*angrily*):   Why should you side with men who break the laws like this?

- Decide on the sound effects you'll introduce to help to tell the story to your listeners, for example, the sounds of a door shutting, or of tea being poured out, or of the sea and of boots crunching on the pebbles of the beach.

Present your script clearly, either for other people to read in a display or for actors to use as they tape the scenes.

Here's a suggested way of doing it. This is a sample layout of the opening of a scene from Part 1 of the story.

> NARRATOR: Presently Lizzy returned to the parlour with her bonnet and cloak on.
>
> LIZZY: (*apologetically*) I am so sorry, but you must help me to get it. Mother has gone to bed. Will you wrap yourself up and come this way, and please bring that cup with you.
>
> NARRATOR: So, Stockdale followed his guide through the garden to the wall.

LIZZY:	It's easy to get up this way.

(Sounds of two thuds as they jump into the church yard – of feet on gravel – of a large key turning in a lock – of a heavy door creaking open)

LIZZY (*confiding*):	You can keep a secret?
STOCKDALE (*fervently and strongly*):	Like an iron chest!

If you've decided to tape the scenes yourselves:

- Rehearse the scripts, remembering what you've learnt about the characters in the story, for example, Lizzy's changing moods, Stockdale's seriousness and anxiety, Owlett's quick thinking and bravery.

- Record the scenes with the sound effects.

Activity 2

In a pair

Read these words, which Lizzy and Stockdale say to each other shortly before Stockdale decides he will have to leave Nether Moynton.

LIZZY:	I cannot do what you wished! It is too much to ask. My whole life has been passed in this way.
STOCKDALE:	I cannot go against my principles in this matter, and I cannot make my profession a mockery.

Together, make two lists:

1 of the reasons why Lizzy cannot give up her life of smuggling

2 of the reasons why Stockdale cannot give up his ministry.

In your pair, take the parts of Lizzy and Stockdale and act out their final, strongly felt argument in your own words, but making use of the reasons you've listed. You could either tape your scene or present it to others and ask for their reactions.

Discuss whether you agree with the choices and decisions each has made. Would it have been better for one or both of them to compromise? Relate their problem to your own experience and observation. Is there anything you would refuse to give up? Is it wrong or right to make compromises?

Working by yourself: thinking and writing

Activity 1: looking at the way Hardy writes

Read the following extract from Part 1 of the story. The numbers link up with some points you'll be asked to comment on after you've finished reading.

At this point in the story, Hardy is helping the reader to see Lizzy Newberry's maturity and experience and Reverend Stockdale's innocence and inexperience. Use the questions to discover some of the ways in which he does this.

As he now lived there, Stockdale felt it unnecessary to knock at the door; and entering quietly he had the pleasure of hearing footsteps scudding away like mice into the back quarters. (1) He advanced to the parlour, as the front room was called, though its stone floor was scarcely disguised by the carpet, which only overlaid the trodden areas, leaving sandy deserts under the furniture. But the room looked *snug and cheerful*. The fire-light shone out brightly, *trembling* on the bulging mouldings of the table-legs, *playing with* brass knobs and handles, and *lurking* in great strength on the under surface of the chimney-piece. (2) A deep arm-chair, covered with horsehair, and studded with a countless throng of brass nails, was pulled up on one side of the fireplace. The tea-things were on the table, the teapot cover was open, and a little hand-bell had been laid at that precise point towards which a person seated in the great chair might be expected instinctively to stretch his hand. (3)

Stockdale sat down, not objecting to his experience of the room thus far, and began his residence by tinkling the bell. A little girl crept in at the summons, and made tea for him. Her name, she said, was Martha Sarer, and she lived out there, nodding towards the road and village generally. Before Stockdale had got far with his meal, a tap sounded on the door behind him, and on his telling the enquirer to come in, a rustle of garments caused him to turn his head. He saw before him a fine and extremely well-made young woman, with dark hair, a wide, sensible, beautiful forehead, eyes that warmed him before he knew it, and a mouth that was in itself a picture to all appreciative souls. (4)

'Can I get you anything else for tea?' she said, coming forward a step or two, an expression of liveliness on her features, and *her hand waving the door by its edge.* (5)

'Nothing, thank you,' said Stockdale, thinking less of what he replied than of what might be her relation to the household.

'You are quite sure?' said the young woman, apparently aware that he had not considered his answer.

He conscientiously (6) examined the tea-things, and found them all there. 'Quite sure, Miss Newberry,' he said.

'It is Mrs. Newberry,' she said. 'Lizzy Newberry. I used to be Lizzy Simpkins.'

'Oh, I beg your pardon, Mrs. Newberry.' And before he had occasion to say more, she left the room.

Stockdale remained in some doubt till Martha Sarah came to clear the table. 'Whose house is this, my little woman?' said he. (7)

'Mrs. Lizzy Newberry's, sir.'

'Then Mrs Newberry is not the old lady I saw this afternoon?'

'No. That's Mrs. Newberry's mother. It was Mrs. Newberry who comed in to you just by now, because she wanted to see if you was good-looking.' (8)

Write your answers to the following questions, as fully as you can.

1   Why do you think Stockdale felt pleasure in 'hearing footsteps scudding away like mice into the back quarters' of the house? What does this make you think about his attitude to his new landlady's household? What does the reader realise is the reason for the 'footsteps scudding away'?

2   Look back at the *italicised* words in the description. What impression of the room, and its owner, do the words help to build up? How do they prepare you for the effect this house and its owner will have on the Reverend Stockdale?

3   You haven't met Lizzy Newberry yet. How do the details in this sentence prepare you for that first meeting? What does she seem to be thinking about her new lodger?

4   In the reader's first meeting with Lizzy, Hardy wants to suggest something about her character as well as about her appearance. From your knowledge of her, which word(s) in this description do you think hint at the character she will show later in the story?

5   This could be a first, polite visit from an efficient landlady. From the *italicised* words, what does the reader realise about the real reasons for her visit?

6   Now look at Lizzy's visit from Stockdale's point of view. What does Hardy's use of the word 'conscientiously' (which means seriously and earnestly) show you about his understanding of the situation?

7   Stockdale already knows Martha Sarah's name, so why does he call her 'my little woman'?

8   When Martha Sarah 'lets the cat out of the bag' with these words, Hardy tells us nothing about Stockdale's reaction to what she says. Write one or two sentences of your own to add to the story at this point, describing his thoughts and feelings. Now that you've written the description, explain, with your reasons, which version is better – yours with the added words, or Hardy's without them.

Activity 2

Hardy tells us about Stockdale's thoughts and feelings, but not Lizzy's.

Re-tell all or part of the story from Lizzy's point of view. You could tell it (i) in the first person, as though Lizzy is talking to the reader, or (ii) in the third person.

Your story could start like this:

(i)

> It was a miserably cold January afternoon when Jim, the carrier's boy, came to ask me if I could take in the new Methodist minister as a lodger. I wasn't sure at first – after all, I'm one of the vicar's congregation in the church – but when I heard that he was young and homeless, my heart softened and I said yes.

(ii)

> On the thirteenth of January 183-, Mrs. Lizzy Newberry took in a lodger, the newly arrived Methodist minister. When the carrier's boy first asked her she was unsure. She wasn't a Methodist and a minister sounded a bit stuffy, but she discovered that he was young and had nowhere to stay, so she said yes.

Activity 3

The smuggler and former miller, Jim Owlett, emigrated to Wisconsin, USA. With his adventurous spirit he may well have become successful and famous there.

Imagine that a local reporter has interviewed Jim about his past life. Write the part of the interview in which Jim talks about his time as a smuggler in Wessex. He would explain how the smuggling was carried out; describe the dangers and excitement of trying to outwit the officers; tell about the part Lizzy played; defend himself against the charge of being called a criminal; and tell the story of his eventual capture.

(If you chose Hardy's preferred ending to the story, you might have decided that Lizzy was with Jim during the interview. She might have joined in.)

Activity 4

In both the two endings to the story, Lizzy's life would have become very different, either in America, many miles from Nether Moynton, or as a minister's wife far from the sea and the countryside in a town in the Midlands.

Decide on the ending you prefer.

Now, think about:

- The differences between her present and her past life.

- The feelings she might have about the changes. For example, does she regret the end of smuggling, or giving up the man she didn't marry?

- How her life has changed as a woman. For example, does she have her own business as she did in Nether Moynton? Will she be restricted by her position as the wife of a minister? For a woman who loved the freedom of wearing men's clothes, how will she dress now, in the 1850s? How might that affect her life?

To help your thoughts, look at the two pictures on page 37, one of young women in 1836 (left), the time at which Hardy set 'The Distracted Preacher', and one of a woman during the late 1850s (right).

Then write the long letter Lizzy composed and sent to Martha Sarah, who has just written from Nether Moynton to tell her about changes in the village. She will write about her present life and her memories of the past, and how she feels about them.

Activity 5

When Hardy called his story 'The Distracted Preacher' he was using the word 'distracted' in two different ways.

- Reverend Stockdale was distracted – put off from what he should have been concentrating on, his work as a minister.

- Reverend Stockdale was distracted – confused and troubled.

Go back to the story and jot down evidence for both the meanings of 'distracted'. If you jotted down notes during your reading, go back to them as well, or remember the discussions you had about the preacher.

Write your account and explanation of how Reverend Stockdale became distracted during the weeks he spent in Nether Moynton. Explain whether you think his experiences have changed him, whether he has 'grown up'.

Activities on both stories

Working with others: talking and dramatising

In a group of three or four

Activity 1

Both the stories have important female characters – Rhoda, Gertrude and Lizzy. In your group, discuss these questions about the three women. Try always to give reasons for the views you express.

- Which of the three women did each of you feel most sympathy with? With which did you feel the least sympathy?

- How do you think Hardy either drew out your sympathy – or turned you against a character?

- What were the chief differences between the lives of the three women? Were there any similarities?

- We saw all three women during the first thirty years of the nineteenth century. What did you discover about the lives of women at that time? For example, how much freedom of choice did they have by comparison with men? How was each of the women treated by men and by the communities they lived in? Do you think Hardy was critical of the way society treated women at that time?

- How different do you think the lives of the three women would have been if they had been living today?

In a group of four

Activity 2

Several of Hardy's short stories and novels have been adapted for film and television.

One director was drawn to Hardy's stories by their:

- strong plot
- modern concerns.

Another by:

- clear construction
- vivid sense of atmosphere
- strong visual effect.

In your group, take each story in turn and discuss whether it shares the features listed by the directors. Would it make a good film?

There are certainly several moments in each story which already seem made for film sequences. Read the list of how four of those sequences might start, and then talk about whether you would add to it any other 'moments' from the stories.

1   The camera follows Farmer Lodge's gig carrying his new wife along the empty, white road towards the setting sun. The boy, the farmer's son, is seen as a 'small scarce-moving speck' in the distance. When the gig catches up with him, the camera looks down at his face as he stares up at Gertrude. A cut to Gertrude's puzzled face and to the farmer's stony expression as he looks ahead and ignores the boy. ('The Withered Arm', Part 2)

2   From inside a small, cell-like room in the gaol, a close-up shot of Gertrude as she comes in and stands by the door; close-up shot of her bare, withered arm supported by her gloved right hand, with the sound of heavy footsteps coming down stairs behind her. Cut to a shot from behind Gertrude, watching four men carry in the coffin and place it on the trestles. Camera follows her as she approaches the coffin. Close-up shot from the opposite side of the coffin, of the hangman uncovering the face and holding Gertrude's arm across the neck. Two shrieks heard as the camera draws back to show Gertrude turned to face Rhoda and Lodge in the doorway. ('The Withered Arm', Part 9)

3   Camera shot from the doorway of Stockdale's bedroom of sunlight coming in through the window and Stockdale waking and stretching with a smile on his face. Camera follows him as he gets out of bed and crosses to the window. Shot down from the window of Lizzy in the garden brushing a muddy greatcoat in the sun. Shot from the garden of Stockdale opening the window, leaning out and calling to Lizzy. Shot from the window of Lizzy turning, looking up at Stockdale, blushing and clumsily rolling up the half-cleaned coat. ('The Distracted Preacher', Part 3)

4   Camera shot of the length of the bell ropes in the church tower and of Stockdale and Lizzy looking upwards to the ceiling. The ladder descends and they climb up towards the trap door. Camera in the belfry gives a close-up of Owlett's anxious face as he and Lizzy talk. Camera follows Stockdale up the second ladder towards the 'pale sky' framed by the trap door leading to the roof of the church tower. Shot from the roof as Stockdale's head emerges, showing in close-up the amazed expressions of villagers lying on the roof. Camera follows Stockdale as he kneels down and peers between the walls of the parapet. Longshot down to the church yard, showing the Customs Officers as 'crablike objects' searching the ground. ('The Distracted Preacher', Part 6)

Choose one of the stories.

Prepare to present for display your filming ideas for:

*   the opening scene of the film

*   the concluding shots in the film

*   two key scenes

*   a poster to advertise the film that will suggest its most dramatic or attractive aspect.

For each scene, discuss and jot down your ideas for:

- the sequence of visual images that will appear on the screen, remembering to indicate camera angles

- the dialogue that the actors will speak in each shot (this could be Hardy's dialogue with additions of your own)

- the sound effects and the kind of music that might accompany the words on the sound track (music and/or sound effects might be particularly effective in setting the atmosphere in the opening scene).

Present your ideas for display as a storyboard and poster.

If you want help with creating a storyboard, look back to the example 'Poem into film' on page 27.

Individual activities Writing

Activity 1

Places were important to Thomas Hardy. The settings of his poems, short stories and novels are always described so that the reader can picture them. He uses the weather, the light, and the memories and Wessex history associated with places to create a mood or atmosphere to suit the happenings and feelings he creates.

Choose:

- two or three poems from the selection at the beginning of this booklet

- one or two scenes from 'The Withered Arm'

- one or two scenes from 'The Distracted Preacher'.

Choose each poem and scene for a place description you think is vivid, and for the mood or atmosphere which you think Hardy has created.

Write:

- an account in your own words of the setting for each poem and scene you've chosen

- an explanation of the mood or atmosphere which the description of the place helps to build up.

Try to pick out and quote any of Hardy's words or short phrases that helped you to form a picture in your mind. Explain what effect the words had on you.

This is the way one reader has written about the scene from Part 7 of 'The Withered Arm' in which Gertrude comes near to the end of her lonely ride to Casterbridge.

> In this scene, Gertrude has been riding on the farm horse across wild Egdon Heath towards Casterbridge. Hardy describes the moment when she reaches the edge of the heath and, instead of seeing moorland all round her, sees the open valley for the first time. She stops by a pool and looks out at the countryside. Hardy describes it as 'low green

country' which helps me to imagine the plain stretching out in front of her. We follow her eyes as she looks over the valley and catches sight of the first houses at the edge of Casterbridge. Then her eyes go up to see a big white building and on the roof some tiny figures moving about. Gertrude then rides down from the heath and through farm land to the edge of the town.

This description helps to build up the suspense and the feelings of Gertrude. We can tell that she stops to look at the countryside and the town in the distance because she is nervous and wants to put off the moment of arriving in Casterbridge for her ordeal. It seems to be a pleasant evening scene until her eyes catch sight of the building. We can imagine it dominating the town when Hardy describes it as a 'white flat facade'. Hardy doesn't explain what is happening on the roof, he just writes that 'specks were moving about, they seemed to be workmen erecting something'. There doesn't need to be any more description, because, like Gertrude, we know that the workmen are putting up the gallows for the hanging. He makes me share her shudder of fear when he writes, 'Her flesh crept'.

Activity 2

Write about the personalities and lives of the three main female characters in the stories: Rhoda, Gertrude, and Lizzy. Compare the three characters, showing how their personalities and lives are similar and how they are different. At the end of your account, explain, with your reasons, how you feel about each of the women. For example, did you like one more than the others? Did you feel sympathy with one, or with all of them? Did you feel satisfied with the ending Hardy gave to each of them in the stories?

Activity 3

Many readers feel Hardy gives a gloomy, pessimistic picture of relationships between men and women. Look back over the stories and the 'love poems' you have read.

Explain whether you agree with these readers. Begin by making lists of reasons for agreeing or disagreeing, noting down evidence from the stories and poems to back up your points. Then write your account, explaining and illustrating each reason in more detail.

Activity 4

Hardy often explained that his own life formed the basis of his short stories and novels. He drew on his childhood experiences, stories about people he'd met, stories people had told him and stories he read in local newspapers.

Look back through this study guide and jot down examples of Hardy's experience that you now know he used as part of the two stories you've been thinking about.

Prepare to write your own story based either on a tale heard from someone else, or on something that has happened to you.

If you've already 'swapped' tales you've been told by older people with your neighbour (look back to the tale-telling activity on page 7), you might have some ideas already. Once Hardy had his idea for starting a story, he would then do research to make sure the details would help readers to understand and picture the action. When he was preparing 'The Withered Arm', he returned to his childhood village to question an elderly woman who had known the 'original' Rhoda Brook. If, for example, you have chosen to write a story based on one of your grandfather's tales of living in the countryside when he was a child, you could talk to him again to find out more. If you are using a memory of your own, talk to a member of your family or a friend who might remember the event in a different and interesting way.

As Hardy did, give new names to your characters and write the story with settings and dialogue so that your readers will be drawn in and involved with the tale you're telling.

Reading the other *Wessex Tales*

By yourself or in a pair

The two stories you've been reading were published first in magazines: 'The Withered Arm' in *Blackwood's Magazine,* January 1888 and 'The Distracted Preacher' in *New Quarterly Magazine*, April 1879. After the success of his early novels and his readers' interest in his created 'country' of Wessex, Hardy put several magazine stories together and called them *Wessex Tales*. The collection was popular enough to be printed three times, in 1888, 1896 and 1912. Like 'The Distracted Preacher' and 'The Withered Arm', the other stories he included are all set in countryside, villages and small towns in the area around Casterbridge – in reality, Dorchester in Dorset. Most of the stories are based on the lives and experiences of country-people Hardy knew or who had featured in the tales he'd heard since childhood. After he had put the final collection together in 1912, Hardy wrote a 'Preface' in which he apologised to his readers because the completed *Wessex Tales* contained 'two stories of hangmen and one of a military execution'.

In their final publication in 1912, there were five other stories:

1   'The Three Strangers'

2   'A Tradition of Eighteen Hundred and Four'

3   'The Melancholy Hussar of the German Legion'

4   'Fellow-Townsmen'

5   'Interlopers at the Knap'.

Take each title in turn and try to predict what might happen and what kind of story it might be – for example; dramatic, tragic, light-hearted, sad?

Read the following extracts from the five stories, which are not in the same order as the story-titles. Then, attempt to match up the extracts with the titles.

A

They brought him nearer the fire, took his hat from his thin hand, which was so small and smooth as to show that his attempts to fetch up again had not been in a manual direction. His mother resumed her inquiries, and dubiously asked if he had chosen to come that particular night for any special reason.

For no reason, he told her. His arrival had been quite at random. Then Philip Hall looked round the room, and saw for the first time that the table was laid somewhat luxuriously, and for a larger number than themselves; and that an air of festivity pervaded their dress. He asked quickly what was going on.

'Sally is going to be married in a day or two,' replied the mother; and she explained how Mr. Darton, Sally's intended husband, was coming there that night with the groomsman, Mr. Johns, and other details. 'We thought it must be their step when we heard you,' said Mrs. Hall.

The needy wanderer looked again on the floor. 'I see – I see,' he murmured. 'Why, indeed, should I have come to-night? Such folk as I are not wanted here at these times, naturally. And I have no business here – spoiling other people's happiness.'

B

While she paused in melancholy regard she fancied that the customary sounds from the tents were changing their character. Indifferent as Phyllis was to camp doings now, she mounted by the steps to the old place. What she beheld at first awed and perplexed her: then she stood rigid, her fingers hooked to the wall, her eyes starting out of her head, and her face as if hardened to stone.

On the open green stretching before her all the regiments in the camp were drawn up in line, in the mid-front of which two empty coffins lay on the ground. The unwonted sounds which she had noticed came from an advancing procession.

C

The shepherd on the east hill could shout out lambing intelligence to the shepherd on the west hill, over the intervening town chimneys, without great inconvenience to his voice, so nearly did the steep pastures encroach upon the burghers' back yards. And at night it was possible to stand in the very midst of the town, and hear from their native paddocks on the lower slopes of greensward the mild lowing of the farmers' heifers, and the profound, warm blowings of breath in which those creatures indulge. But the community which had jammed itself in the valley thus flanked formed a veritable town, with a real mayor and corporation, and a staple manufacture. During a certain damp evening five-and-thirty years ago, before the twilight was far advanced, a pedestrian of professional appearance, carrying a small bag in his hand and an elevated umbrella, was descending one of these hills by the turnpike road when he was overtaken by a phaeton.

'Hullo, Downe – is that you?' said the driver of the vehicle, a young man of pale and refined appearance. 'Jump up here with me, and ride down to your door.'

D

'By and by we drew up to the fold, saw that all was right, and then, to keep ourselves warm, curled up in a heap of straw that lay inside the thatched hurdles we had set up to break the stroke of the wind when there was any …

'While we lay there Uncle Job amused me by telling me strange stories of the wars he had served in and the wounds he had got. He had already fought the French in the Low Countries, and hoped to fight 'em again. His stories lasted so long that at last I was hardly sure that I was not a soldier myself, and had seen such service as he told of. The wonders of his tales quite bewildered my mind, till I fell asleep and dreamed of battle, smoke, and flying soldiers, all of a kind with the doings he had been bringing up to me.

'How long my nap lasted I am not prepared to say. But some faint sounds over and above the rustle of the ewes in the straw, the bleat of the lambs, and the tinkle of the sheep-bell brought me to my waking senses. Uncle Job was still beside me; but he too had fallen asleep. I looked out from the straw, and saw what it was that had aroused me. Two men, in boat-cloaks, cocked hats, and swords, stood by the hurdles about twenty yards off.'

E

The stranger in cinder-gray took no notice of this whispered string of observations, but again wetted his lips. Seeing that his friend in the chimney-corner was the only one who reciprocated his joviality in any way, he held out his cup towards that appreciative comrade, who also held out his own. They clicked together, the eyes of the rest of the room hanging upon the singer's actions. He parted his lips for the third verse; but at that moment another knock was audible upon the door. This time the knock was faint and hesitating.

The company seemed scared; the shepherd looked with consternation towards the entrance, and it was with some effort that he resisted his alarmed wife's deprecatory glance, and uttered for the third time the welcoming words, 'Walk in!'

The door was gently opened, and another man stood upon the mat. He, like those who had preceded him, was a stranger. This time it was a short small personage, of fair complexion, and dressed in a decent suit of dark clothes.

'Can you tell me the way to—?'

Check your order with the correct order. The answers can be found on page 48.

Re-read each extract. Jot down or discuss what more you can predict about each story. Can you identify, for example:

- which is the other story that features a hangman?

- the one including a military execution?

Are any of the stories going to be humorous, or about love, or about a mystery?

Now, read as many of the stories as you can, and discover whether your predictions have been right.

Connections

Other short stories by Thomas Hardy

If you have completed the previous activity, you will have discovered something about the other stories that, with those you have read and studied, make up the *Wessex Tales*. These are the editions of *Wessex Tales* now in print:

Wessex Tales, Amerson Ltd, 1976

Wessex Tales, World's Classics (Oxford), 1991

Wessex Tales, Wordsworth, 1998

There are other short stories written by Hardy that you might enjoy and that pick up ideas, situations and feelings you have already become familiar with in the poems and stories you have worked on. Here are some suggestions:

'A Mere Interlude'

'Barbara of the House of Grebe'

'On the Western Circuit'

'The Son's Veto'

'The Fiddler of the Reels'

You will find a range of stories in the following collections:

The Fiddler of the Reels and Other Stories, Dover Thrift, 1997

The Distracted Preacher and Other Stories, Penguin Classics, 1996

An Indiscretion in the Life of an Heiress and Other Stories, Oxford World's Classics, 1995

Selected Short Stories, Wordsworth Classics, 1998

Selected Short Stories and Poems, Everyman, 1993

Making connections with short stories by other writers

You might enjoy other short stories written by authors during the nineteenth century. Those suggested explore some of the themes you have thought about in reading 'The Withered Arm' and 'The Distracted Preacher' – relationships between men and women, mystery and punishment:

Dickens, Charles, 'The Signalman'

Kipling, Rudyard, 'Cupid's Arrows', 'Beyond the Pale', 'In the Pride of his Youth', in *Plain Tales from the Hills*, Wordsworth, 1993

Trollope, Anthony, 'The Parson's Daughter of Oxney Colne', 'Malachi's Cove', in *The Collected Shorter Fiction,* Robinson Publishing, 1992

Twentieth-century writers of short stories have often explored the themes of love and relationships between men and women. Try to read several stories from the following list and think, and perhaps write, about similarities and differences in the ways Hardy and these later authors explore the subject:

Callaghan, Morley, 'It Must Be Different', in *Stories 11*, MacGibbon and Kee, and in the school anthology, *It Must Be Different*, B. Newton (ed.), Collins, 1983

Daly, Maureen, 'I Remember You', in *Sixteen and Other Stories*, Dodd, Mead and Co., and in the school anthology, *Love Stories*, John L. Foster (ed.), Ward Lock, 1975

Geras, Adele, 'Tea in the Wendy House', in *The Green behind the Glass*, Collins, and in the school anthology, *Frankie Mae and Other Stories*, A. Mann and H. Rich (eds), Nelson, 1987

Lawrence, D.H., 'Tickets Please', in *The Complete Short Stories*, Heinemann, and in the school anthology, *Modern Short Stories*, J. Hunter (ed.), Faber, 1964

MacLaverty, Bernard, 'My Dear Palestrina', in *A Time to Dance*, Jonathan Cape, and in the school anthology, *The Best of Bernard MacLaverty*, Heinemann Windmill, 1990

Naughton, Bill, 'Taking a Beauty Queen Home', in *Late Night on Watling Street*, Longman, 1972

Vonnegut, Kurt, 'Long Walk to Forever', in *Welcome to the Monkey House*, Delacourt/Seymour Lawrence, and in the school anthology, *It Must Be Different*, B. Newton (ed.), Collins, 1983

Novels by Thomas Hardy

These are the most famous of Hardy's novels, listed in the order he wrote them. Now that you have read *Wessex Tales*, you might enjoy any of these longer stories:

Under the Greenwood Tree, 1872

Far from the Madding Crowd, 1874

The Return of the Native, 1878

The Trumpet Major, 1880

The Mayor of Casterbridge, 1886

The Woodlanders, 1887

Tess of the D'Urbervilles, 1891

Jude the Obscure, 1896

Thomas Hardy's stories on screen

Many of Hardy's stories have been filmed, some more than once. Several of the films or television serial versions are available on video:

Far from the Madding Crowd	film (1967) and ITV serial (1998)
The Return of the Native	ITV film (1994)
The Mayor of Casterbridge	BBC serial (1978)
The Woodlanders	film (1997)
Tess of the D'Urbervilles	film (1981) and ITV film (1997)

Jude the Obscure　　　　　　　　　film (1996) and BBC serial (1971)

The Scarlet Tunic　　　　　　　　　film (1998)
(an adaptation of 'The Melancholy Hussar')

Research　If you would like to discover more about Thomas Hardy, his life, the times he lived through and the places that inspired him, these are suggested sources for your research.

Organisations

The Thomas Hardy Society, PO Box 1438, Dorchester, Dorset

Dorset County Museum, High West Street, Dorchester, Dorset

Books

Fowles, John, and Draper, Jo, *Thomas Hardy's England*, Jonathan Cape, 1984

Gittings, Robert, *Young Thomas Hardy*, Penguin, 1975

Lefebure, Molly, *Thomas Hardy's World*, Carlton, 1996

Pinion, F.B., *A Hardy Companion*, Macmillan, 1968

Web sites

The Thomas Hardy Resource Library:
　　　　　　　　http://pages.ripco.com:8080/~mws/hardy.html

The Thomas Hardy Association:
　　　　　　　　http://www.yale.edu/hardysoc/Welcome/welcomet.htm

Thomas Hardy Photo Archive:
　　　　　　　　http://home.att.net/~bwmartin/Hardy_Home.htm

The Thomas Hardy Miscellany:
　　　　　　　　http://www.andover.edu/english/hardymisc

Thomas Hardy On-line Society:
　　　　　　　　http://www.prestigeweb.com/hardy/hardy.html

Dorset Library Service – Thomas Hardy Collection:
　　　　　　　　http://www.dorset-cc.gov.uk/hardycol.htm

Answers to activity on pages 44–5
(1 – E, 2 – D, 3 – B, 4 – C, 5 – A)